Flipping Houses Like Pro

Master the Latest Strategies and Practical Steps for Profitable Investments

Ghazwan Alemara

Copyright © 2024 Ghazwan Alemara. All rights reserved.

No part of this publication may be reproduced, distributed, or transmitted in any form or by any means, including photocopying, recording, or other electronic or mechanical methods, without the prior written permission of the publisher, except in the case of brief quotations embodied in critical reviews and certain other noncommercial uses permitted by copyright law.

For permissions requests or inquiries, please contact the publisher at hello@ghazwanalemara.com

Published by ghazwanalemara.com

Contents

Contents 3
Introduction 1
The Foundations of Flipping 4
    Understanding What Flipping Houses Really Means 4
    The Pros and Cons of Flipping 6
    The Golden Rules of Flipping 10
Getting Started – Your First Flip 13
    Assessing Your Financial Readiness 13
    Finding the Right Market 15
    Starting Small – Your First Project 19
Financing Your Flip 22
    Securing Funding for Your Investment 22
    Creative Financing Options 24
    Budgeting and Contingencies 27
Finding the Perfect Property 30
    Sourcing Deals 30
    Evaluating Properties for Flipping 33
    Avoiding Common Mistakes When Buying 36
The Renovation Process 39
    Creating a Renovation Plan 39
    Working with Contractors 41
    DIY vs. Professional Work 43
Selling for Maximum Profit 46
    Staging Your Home to Sell Fast 46

 Pricing Your Flip 50
 Working with Real Estate Agents 52
Advanced Strategies for Scaling Your Business 55
 Transitioning from Hobbyist to Professional Flipper 55
 Building a Team of Experts 57
 Leveraging Technology and Data 59
Legal and Tax Considerations 63
 Legal Issues in House Flipping 63
 Tax Implications 66
 When Flipping Becomes a Business 68
Common Pitfalls and How to Avoid Them 72
 Overestimating Profit Margins 72
 Market Fluctuations 74
 Staying Emotionally Detached 76
Conclusion 79

Introduction

Imagine standing outside a once-neglected house. The paint is peeling, the windows are cracked, and the overgrown lawn has seen better days. But instead of seeing disrepair, you see potential—potential to turn this rundown property into a shining gem and, more importantly, a profitable investment. That's the art of flipping houses, and it's an art that, with the right tools, you can master.

Flipping houses has long captured the imagination of aspiring investors, creative problem-solvers, and anyone looking to build wealth outside the traditional 9-to-5 grind. But behind the success stories of quick profits and eye-catching transformations lies a field filled with challenges and risks. It's not just about picking up a hammer or choosing paint colors. It's about understanding the market, knowing when to take calculated risks, and mastering the latest strategies that can turn any property into a worthwhile investment.

In this book you'll learn how to do just that. Whether you're brand new to flipping or looking to sharpen your skills, this book will walk you through the entire process—from finding your first property to cashing in on a successful sale. The goal is simple: to equip you with the tools, techniques, and mindset needed to succeed in today's competitive real estate market.

Why does this matter now more than ever? Flipping houses isn't just about making a quick buck; it's about adapting to a constantly shifting market, seizing opportunities, and making informed decisions that set you up for long-term success. In recent years, the rise of new technologies, economic changes, and shifting buyer preferences have transformed the real estate landscape. The strategies that worked a decade ago won't cut it in today's market, which is why this book emphasizes the latest techniques—from financing and budgeting to sourcing properties and handling renovations.

We'll begin with the fundamentals of house flipping, ensuring that even beginners have a solid understanding of the key principles. Then, we'll dive into financing, where you'll discover the different ways to fund your flips, whether you're using your own money or borrowing from investors. Next, we'll explore the renovation process, offering practical tips on everything from hiring contractors to managing a renovation budget. The book will guide you through marketing and selling your flip for maximum profit, and for those ready to scale their operations, we'll cover advanced strategies for building a long-term flipping business.

Through real-world examples, case studies, and actionable steps, you'll gain insights that go beyond the basics. You'll understand how to read the market, avoid common pitfalls, and flip with confidence, even in uncertain economic times. With this knowledge, you'll not only be able to profit from individual flips but also turn flipping houses into a sustainable business.

Whether you're looking to flip houses as a side hustle or aiming to turn it into a full-time career, the strategies outlined in this book will help you unlock the doors to success. So, get ready to embark on this journey with me. By the end of this book, you'll have the skills and knowledge to flip houses like a pro—and more importantly, you'll be well on your way to building the life and financial freedom you've always dreamed of.

Chapter 1

The Foundations of Flipping

Understanding What Flipping Houses Really Means

Flipping houses has become a buzzword in real estate, but what does it truly mean? At its core, flipping houses is about purchasing a property with the intention of reselling it for a profit. The process is relatively simple in theory: you find a home, fix it up, and sell it for more than you paid. But as with any business, the reality is much more nuanced.

To truly understand flipping, you need to look beyond just buying and selling. It's a strategy that requires a mix of skills—negotiation, renovation, and market analysis, to name a few. And unlike traditional real estate investments, where you might buy a property and hold onto it for years, flipping is all about speed. The faster you can turn the property around, the better, because every day you own it, you're paying for things like mortgage interest, taxes, and utilities.

At its heart, flipping houses is an investment strategy that relies on creating value. You're not just hoping the market will improve (although that helps); you're actively adding value to the property through renovations, repairs, and upgrades. This can mean anything from updating the kitchen and bathrooms to fixing structural issues or enhancing the home's curb appeal. The goal is to transform a property into something more desirable, making it attractive to potential buyers and increasing its resale value.

Flipping also requires a deep understanding of your local market. You can't just buy any home and expect to flip it for a profit. Successful flippers know how to spot properties that are priced below market value—perhaps because they need repairs or have been on the market too long—and have the vision to see what those homes could become. It's about recognizing potential where others might not.

Another key aspect of flipping is timing. The real estate market is always shifting, and what might be a great deal today could be a losing proposition tomorrow. A big part of flipping is knowing when to buy and, just as importantly, when to sell. This involves staying on top of market trends, understanding seasonal fluctuations, and keeping a close eye on economic indicators that can affect housing prices.

In the end, flipping houses is about turning opportunity into profit. It's not a get-rich-quick scheme, despite what TV shows may portray. It requires a careful balancing act of buying smart, investing in the right renovations, and selling at the optimal time. When done well, flipping can be incredibly rewarding, both financially and creatively. You get to transform spaces, breathe new life into neglected homes, and make a tangible impact on the real estate market—all while turning a profit.

Before and After Flip Transformation. Source: youtube.com

The Pros and Cons of Flipping

Flipping houses can be an exciting and lucrative venture, but it's not without its challenges. Like any investment, it comes with its share of risks and rewards, and understanding both sides is essential before diving in. Let's explore the advantages and disadvantages of flipping houses so you can decide if it's the right path for you.

One of the most attractive aspects of flipping is the potential for quick profits. Unlike other real estate investments, which can take years to yield significant returns, a well-executed flip can generate a substantial profit in a matter of months. If you're skilled at identifying undervalued properties and have the ability to manage a renovation efficiently, the rewards can be significant.

Flipping houses also offers a unique opportunity for creativity. You're not just making financial decisions; you're transforming a space. For those with a keen eye for design or a passion for renovation, the process of turning a rundown property into a desirable home can be deeply satisfying. It's a chance to bring a vision to life, one that adds value to the neighborhood and provides a beautiful home for future buyers.

In addition to creative fulfillment, flipping houses can offer a flexible lifestyle. Many successful flippers treat it as a full-time career, while others do it part-time or alongside other ventures. If you're someone who enjoys working on your own schedule or values the independence that comes with entrepreneurship, flipping houses can provide that freedom.

There's also the thrill of beating the market. In real estate, the potential to buy low and sell high is always enticing. By understanding market trends, finding the right property, and timing your sale well, you can significantly outpace returns from more traditional investments like stocks or bonds.

While the rewards are tempting, the risks should not be underestimated. Perhaps the biggest drawback of flipping houses is the unpredictability of the market. Even if you purchase a property at a great price and complete a successful renovation, there's no guarantee that the housing market will remain stable. If market conditions take a downturn while you're holding the property, you could be forced to sell at a loss or hold onto it much longer than anticipated.

Another challenge is the upfront capital required. Flipping houses isn't cheap, and beyond the initial cost of the property, you'll need to budget for renovations, carrying costs like taxes and insurance, and unexpected expenses that inevitably arise. Access to financing, whether through personal savings, loans, or investors, is crucial, and even with the right resources, things can get tight if a flip doesn't go according to plan.

The renovation process itself can be a double-edged sword. While it's exciting to improve a property, managing a renovation can be stressful and time-consuming. Delays are common, contractors may go over budget, and unexpected problems like structural issues or outdated wiring can quickly eat into your profits. Renovation projects often look straightforward on paper, but once you're in the thick of it, they can become much more complicated.

Additionally, flipping houses involves tax implications that can cut into your profits. Depending on how quickly you flip a property and where you're located, you could be subject to higher short-term capital gains taxes. Flipping properties also requires a strong grasp of local laws and regulations, as zoning rules, building codes, and permits all play a critical role in your success.

Finally, flipping houses requires a great deal of time and effort. While it can offer flexibility, it's far from passive income. You'll need to devote significant time to finding properties, managing renovations, handling legal and financial matters, and selling the property. For those looking for a quick or easy way to make money, flipping houses is unlikely to deliver. It's a hands-on process that demands both time and energy, and success is far from guaranteed.

Flipping houses can be a rewarding endeavor for those willing to navigate the ups and downs. The potential for profit is real, but it requires careful planning, a good understanding of the market, and a willingness to put in the hard work. Knowing both the pros and cons of flipping is the first step to determining if this path is the right one for you.

The Golden Rules of Flipping

Flipping houses can be incredibly rewarding, but success doesn't happen by accident. The most successful flippers follow a set of principles that guide their decisions and help them avoid costly mistakes. If you're serious about making money through flipping, it's important to understand and stick to these rules.

First and foremost, you must buy at the right price. This is perhaps the most crucial rule of all. The profit in flipping is made when you buy, not when you sell. If you overpay for a property, it can be almost impossible to make a decent profit, no matter how well you renovate it. The key is to find properties priced below market value, usually because they need significant repairs or have been neglected. Once you find the right deal, you have a much better chance of making the numbers work in your favor.

Another golden rule is to budget conservatively. Flipping involves a lot of moving parts: materials, labor, permits, and more, and costs can add up quickly. Even with careful planning, unexpected expenses almost always pop up. Whether it's a plumbing issue no one noticed or a delay in the renovation schedule, you need to have a financial cushion to cover the unexpected. Always assume things will cost more than you think and take longer than you plan. This way, you're prepared when things don't go exactly as planned.

Timing is also critical. The longer you hold onto a property, the more it costs you. Monthly expenses like mortgage payments, property taxes, insurance, and utilities start to eat into your profit margins the moment you close on the property. That's why it's important to move quickly, but not recklessly. A well-planned renovation and efficient execution are key to getting the property back on the market as fast as possible. However, rushing the process at the expense of quality can backfire, so balance speed with precision.

Understanding your market is another rule that successful flippers swear by. Real estate markets can vary widely from one neighborhood to another, even within the same city. What sells in one area might sit for months in another. Before you even consider buying a property, you need to know what buyers in that area are looking for. Are homes with open-concept kitchens in demand? Do buyers prioritize energy efficiency or smart home technology? The more you know about your local market, the better equipped you'll be to make smart decisions about which upgrades will yield the highest returns.

Lastly, stay emotionally detached from the property. Flipping is a business, and emotional decisions can lead to overspending or holding onto a property for too long. You might fall in love with the home you're working on, but remember, it's not for you. It's for the buyer. Keep a clear focus on the end goal: creating a home that will sell quickly for the best possible price.

By following these golden rules—buying smart, budgeting conservatively, timing your flip well, knowing your market, and staying emotionally detached—you set yourself up for success in the world of house flipping. These principles, while simple, can make the difference between a profitable flip and one that drains your time and resources.

Chapter 2

Getting Started – Your First Flip

Assessing Your Financial Readiness

Before jumping into house flipping, it's crucial to take an honest look at your financial situation. Flipping requires a significant upfront investment, and being financially prepared can mean the difference between success and stress. Even if you've found the perfect property at a great price, if your finances aren't in order, the project could quickly spiral out of control.

First, you need to determine how much capital you have available. This includes not just the money you plan to use to purchase the property, but also the funds required for renovations, holding costs, and unexpected expenses. Many first-time flippers make the mistake of underestimating the true costs involved, thinking only of the purchase price and basic renovation expenses. However, flipping a house comes with additional costs like property taxes, insurance, utilities, and sometimes interest on loans. It's important to ensure that you have enough financial padding to cover these expenses while still leaving room for profit.

If you don't have the entire amount in cash, you'll need to explore financing options. Traditional mortgage loans may not always be the best fit for flipping, as they often have longer approval times and may not cover renovation costs. Many flippers turn to hard money loans, which are short-term, high-interest loans that can be secured quickly but come with the expectation of faster repayment. While these loans offer flexibility, it's essential to understand the costs associated with them and ensure that you can repay them within the set timeline.

It's also important to evaluate your credit score and debt-to-income ratio. Lenders look at these factors when determining whether you qualify for a loan and at what interest rate. A lower credit score or high levels of existing debt could make it more difficult to secure financing or lead to higher borrowing costs, which will eat into your profits.

Another key part of financial readiness is assessing your risk tolerance. Flipping houses involves a level of risk, and you should be prepared for the possibility that the project may not go exactly as planned. Markets fluctuate, renovations can exceed budgets, and selling a property may take longer than expected. If you're the type of person who would be highly stressed by these variables, it's essential to weigh whether this is the right path for you. Having a financial cushion to absorb unexpected setbacks can make the process much smoother.

Ultimately, flipping houses isn't just about having enough money to buy and fix up a property. It's about ensuring you have a complete financial plan in place to manage every aspect of the project. From securing the right financing to preparing for hidden costs and market shifts, understanding your financial readiness is the first critical step toward flipping successfully.

Finding the Right Market

One of the most important decisions you'll make as a house flipper is choosing the right market to invest in. The market you select can determine whether your flip is a success or a struggle. Even the best renovation can't save a flip if the market conditions aren't in your favor.

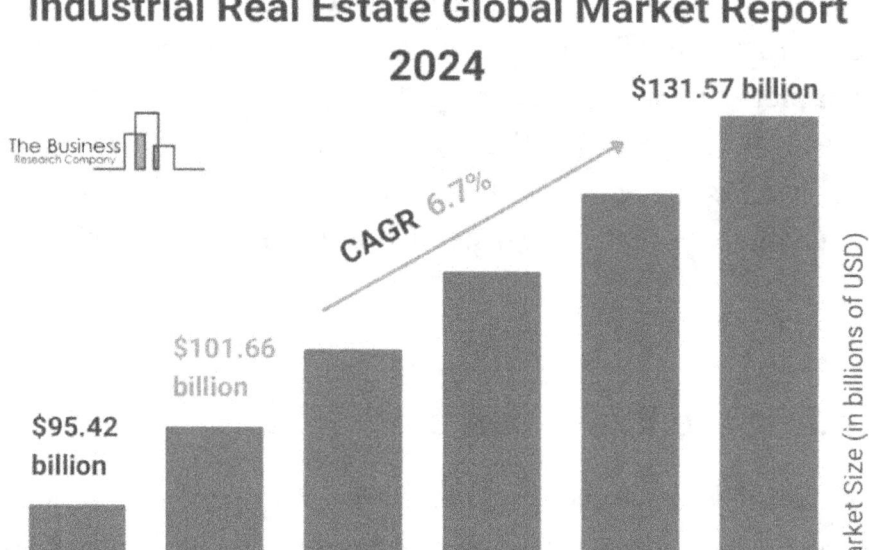

Industrial Real Estate Market Growth Projection (2023–2028). Source: thebusinessresearchcompany.com

The first step to finding the right market is understanding local demand. Some areas have a higher demand for homes than others, and this demand will directly impact how quickly and for how much you can sell your flip. Start by looking at cities or neighborhoods that are growing. A growing population often means more buyers, which increases the chance that your property will sell quickly. Pay attention to trends like new job opportunities in the area or upcoming infrastructure projects, such as new schools or public transportation, which can make a neighborhood more attractive to buyers.

Location is critical in real estate, and that's especially true for flipping houses. You want to target neighborhoods where homes are selling quickly but where there's still potential to find properties at a price that makes sense for flipping. A market that's too hot may not leave enough room for profit, as prices could be too high to find a good deal. On the other hand, a market with very low demand could mean your flip will sit unsold for months. Aim for neighborhoods that are on the rise but haven't yet peaked in terms of home values. These "up-and-coming" areas often offer the best opportunities for flippers.

Another key factor is competition. While it's great to find a market with high demand, too much competition from other flippers or investors can make it difficult to find a good deal. If every property that hits the market gets multiple offers right away, you may find yourself overpaying just to get in on the action. Look for markets where you can still find distressed properties, foreclosures, or homes that have been sitting on the market for a while. These are often the best deals for flippers since they offer more room for negotiation.

It's also essential to consider the type of buyer in the area. Different markets attract different kinds of buyers, and knowing who your target buyer is will help you decide how to approach your flip. For example, some neighborhoods may attract young professionals who are looking for modern, stylish homes with lots of upgrades. Other areas might be more appealing to families who are focused on good school districts and outdoor space. Understanding what buyers in your market want can guide your renovation decisions, ensuring that you make upgrades that will appeal to them and increase your chances of a quick sale.

Finally, do your homework on local regulations and taxes. Every market has its own set of rules and costs associated with real estate transactions. Some areas have higher property taxes, while others may have stricter rules about renovations and permits. These costs can eat into your profits if you're not careful. Make sure you understand what it takes to buy, renovate, and sell a house in the market you're targeting before you commit.

Finding the right market is a balance of research, timing, and understanding the local real estate dynamics. With careful consideration, you can choose a market that maximizes your chances for success and sets your flip on the path to profitability.

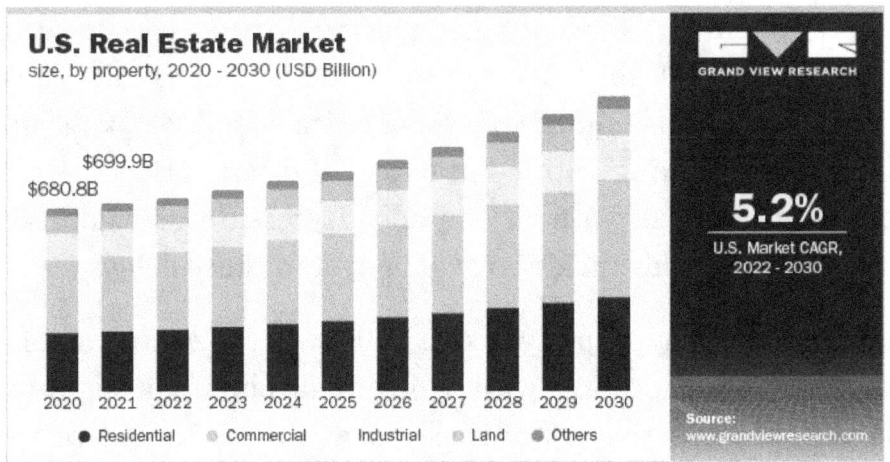

U.S. Real Estate Market Trends (2020–2030). Source: grandviewresearch.com

Starting Small – Your First Project

When you're new to flipping houses, starting small is one of the best decisions you can make. It's tempting to dive into a large project that promises huge profits, but taking on too much too soon can overwhelm even the most determined beginner. A smaller, more manageable project allows you to learn the ropes without taking on unnecessary risks.

Your first project should be about gaining experience, not making a fortune. Look for a property that needs cosmetic updates rather than major structural repairs. Cosmetic improvements, like painting, replacing fixtures, or updating flooring, are typically less expensive and easier to handle. These types of projects allow you to practice essential skills like budgeting, working with contractors, and navigating the real estate market, all without the added pressure of significant repairs that could quickly go over budget or cause delays.

Finding the right property is key. You'll want to choose a home that's in a good location, with strong resale potential, but not so large or complex that it stretches your abilities. Many successful first-time flippers start with homes in stable, middle-income neighborhoods where demand is consistent. The ideal property is one that needs just enough work to add value, but not so much that it becomes a money pit.

Working with a smaller budget on your first flip also helps you develop financial discipline. It forces you to make smart choices about where to spend your money and how to get the most value out of each renovation. You'll quickly learn how to prioritize improvements that will have the biggest impact on the home's value, such as kitchens and bathrooms, without getting caught up in expensive details that won't necessarily lead to higher profits.

Starting with a smaller project also allows you to build a team you can rely on for future flips. You'll get to know contractors, real estate agents, and other professionals who can help guide you through the process. Establishing these relationships early on is invaluable as you grow your flipping business.

The key to your first project is to focus on learning and gaining confidence. You're building the foundation for future success, and a smaller project will help you make mistakes that you can afford to learn from. Once you've completed your first flip, you'll have a much clearer idea of what flipping involves and how to manage larger, more complex projects with greater potential for profit.

Chapter 3

Financing Your Flip

Securing Funding for Your Investment

Before you can start flipping houses, you'll need to figure out how to secure the funding for your investment. Flipping houses requires capital, not only to buy the property but also to cover the cost of renovations, holding expenses, and any unexpected issues that might arise. Fortunately, there are several ways to finance a flip, depending on your situation and goals.

One of the most common methods of funding a flip is through a traditional mortgage. This works well if you have a strong credit history, a steady income, and can make a down payment. Mortgages generally offer lower interest rates compared to other forms of financing, making them attractive if you plan to hold onto the property for a few months while completing renovations. However, the approval process for a mortgage can be slow, and lenders may not always look favorably on properties that need significant repairs. If time is of the essence, this might not be the best option for every flip.

For those looking for faster access to funds, hard money loans can be an appealing choice. Hard money lenders are typically private investors or companies that specialize in providing short-term loans for real estate investments. These loans are based more on the value of the property than on your personal financial history, which means they can be easier to qualify for. However, they often come with higher interest rates and shorter repayment terms. While hard money loans can be a great tool for quick flips, it's important to factor in the costs and make sure your projected profit margin can handle the added expense.

Another option is to work with private lenders. Private lenders can be individuals—friends, family members, or other investors—who are willing to loan you money to finance your flip. These agreements tend to be more flexible than traditional mortgages or hard money loans, with terms that are negotiable between you and the lender. The downside is that you'll need to find someone willing to invest in your project, and this often requires building trust and demonstrating your ability to deliver a solid return.

If you're not looking to take on debt, you might consider pooling resources with other investors. Partnering with an investor or group of investors allows you to share the costs and risks of the flip while splitting the profits. In this scenario, you might provide the expertise and oversee the project, while your partner provides the funding. This can be a great way to get started in flipping if you don't have enough capital on your own, but it also means sharing the reward once the property is sold.

For those with some experience or larger networks, crowdfunding platforms are another way to raise funds. Real estate crowdfunding has grown in popularity in recent years, allowing you to raise money from multiple investors to fund your flip. These platforms connect flippers with investors who are interested in real estate, creating an opportunity to access funds without going through traditional lending channels. Each platform has its own structure and fees, so it's important to understand how they work before diving in.

No matter which route you choose, securing funding for a flip requires careful planning. It's crucial to know your budget inside and out, including purchase price, renovation costs, holding costs, and any fees associated with financing. Having a clear plan not only helps you secure the funding you need but also ensures that you're well-prepared to make your flip a financial success.

Creative Financing Options

When it comes to flipping houses, not everyone has the cash on hand to purchase a property outright. Fortunately, there are a variety of creative financing options that can help you get started without draining your savings. These methods can open doors to new opportunities, allowing you to invest in properties even if traditional bank loans aren't an option for you.

One popular approach is partnering with private investors. Instead of going through a bank, you can connect with individuals who are interested in real estate but may not have the time or expertise to flip houses themselves. In this arrangement, you typically provide the time and effort, while they provide the capital. The profits are then split based on the agreement you've made. This option allows you to leverage someone else's money while sharing the risk and reward.

Seller financing is another creative option worth considering. In this scenario, the seller of the property agrees to finance the purchase instead of you going through a traditional lender. Essentially, the seller acts as the bank, and you make monthly payments directly to them. This can be a great option if you find a motivated seller who is willing to be flexible, especially if the property has been on the market for a while or needs significant repairs. Seller financing can also speed up the transaction, as there's no need to wait for bank approval.

Hard money loans are a more common option for house flippers. These loans come from private lenders and are typically short-term, high-interest loans designed specifically for investment properties. The major advantage of hard money loans is that they are based on the value of the property rather than your credit score. This means they can be easier to qualify for if the deal is right. However, the interest rates and fees are usually higher than traditional loans, so it's essential to ensure the numbers work before taking this route.

Another strategy is using a home equity loan or line of credit (HELOC). If you own your home or another property with equity built up, you can borrow against that equity to fund your flip. A HELOC gives you access to a revolving line of credit that can be used for the purchase and renovation costs. This option typically comes with lower interest rates compared to other creative financing methods, but you'll need to be careful not to over-leverage your primary home.

Crowdfunding is a newer but growing trend in real estate investing. Platforms now exist where multiple investors can pool their money together to fund a property flip. This allows you to raise the necessary capital from a larger group of people, each contributing a smaller amount. Crowdfunding can be an attractive option if you have a solid business plan but lack access to traditional funding sources.

Creative financing allows you to think outside the box and find solutions that fit your specific needs. Whether you're working with private investors, exploring seller financing, or leveraging hard money loans, these options can help you move forward with your flip even if your personal finances aren't ready to handle the full cost upfront. Each method has its own advantages and risks, so it's important to choose the one that aligns best with your project and financial goals.

Budgeting and Contingencies

When flipping houses, having a well-planned budget is crucial to ensuring your project stays profitable. Many first-time flippers make the mistake of focusing only on the purchase price and renovation costs, but successful budgeting goes beyond that. A thorough budget includes every expense you're likely to encounter, from the obvious to the unexpected.

Start by estimating your renovation costs. This includes everything from materials and labor to permits and inspections. Be as specific as possible when calculating these costs, and don't forget to account for the little things, like fixtures and finishes, that can add up quickly. Getting quotes from contractors and suppliers early on will help you create a realistic estimate.

Next, factor in your holding costs. These are the expenses you'll need to cover while you own the property, such as property taxes, utilities, insurance, and loan payments. The longer it takes to complete the renovation and sell the house, the more these costs will eat into your profit. It's a good idea to overestimate how long you'll be holding the property, just in case things take longer than expected.

One of the most important elements of your budget is the contingency fund. No matter how well you plan, unexpected issues are almost guaranteed to come up during a flip. Maybe you discover mold behind a wall, or a plumbing issue requires more extensive repairs than you anticipated. Without a contingency fund, these surprises can throw off your entire budget and leave you scrambling to cover the extra costs. A good rule of thumb is to set aside 10 to 20 percent of your renovation budget for contingencies. This gives you a financial cushion to handle any surprises without derailing the project.

It's also essential to track your spending throughout the project. As renovations progress, keep a close eye on your expenses to ensure you're staying within your budget. If certain areas start to go over budget, you may need to adjust other parts of the project to make up the difference. Being flexible and willing to make adjustments is key to staying on track financially.

A well-structured budget, along with a healthy contingency fund, provides the foundation for a successful flip. It not only helps you plan for expected costs but also prepares you for the unexpected, reducing stress and ensuring your flip stays profitable even when challenges arise.

Profit and Loss Statement	Flip in 8 months	Flip in 12 months
Net Revenue		
Expected Sale Price	$320,000	$320,000
- Purchase Price	$275,000	$275,000
- Selling Costs	$15,450	$15,450
Net Revenue	**$29,550**	**$29,550**
General Expenses		
Acquisition Costs	$6,350	$6,350
Renovations	$22,300	$22,300
Interest Expenses	$6,651	$9,950
Housing Expenses	$3,960	$5,940
Total Expenses	**$39,261**	**$44,540**
Profit / Loss	-$9,711	-$14,990
Estimated Taxes	$0	$0
Net Income	**-$9,711**	**-$14,990**

Profit and Loss Scenarios: Flip in 8 Months vs. 12 Months. Source: businesscaseguy.com

Chapter 4

Finding the Perfect Property

Sourcing Deals

Finding the right deals is one of the most important steps in the house-flipping process. A great deal sets the stage for a successful flip, while a poor one can lead to frustration and financial loss. The key to sourcing deals is knowing where to look and staying persistent in your search.

One of the most common ways to find properties for flipping is through the Multiple Listing Service (MLS). This is a database that real estate agents use to list properties for sale. While this is a highly accessible option, keep in mind that properties on the MLS are available to everyone, which can drive up competition. Still, with the right strategy, you can find undervalued or distressed properties that others might overlook. It's important to work with a real estate agent who understands your goals and can alert you to new listings quickly.

Another approach is attending property auctions. Properties that end up at auction are often foreclosures or homes with unpaid taxes. Auctions can offer some of the best deals, but they come with a certain level of risk. Many times, you won't have the chance to inspect the property thoroughly before bidding, which means you could end up with more repairs than you expected. It's essential to do as much research as possible before attending an auction, such as driving by the property or reviewing public records for any major issues.

Off-market deals can also be a goldmine for house flippers. These are properties that aren't listed on the open market, which means there's less competition from other buyers. To find off-market deals, you might need to network with other real estate professionals, such as agents, contractors, and property managers, who can tip you off when they come across a property that might be for sale. You can also try direct-to-seller marketing, such as sending letters or postcards to property owners who might be interested in selling but haven't yet listed their home. This approach takes time and effort, but it can yield excellent opportunities.

Another option is working with wholesalers. Wholesalers specialize in finding properties at a discount and then selling them to investors like you for a small markup. They do the legwork of finding motivated sellers, negotiating a deal, and assigning the contract to you. This can save you time, but be sure to factor in the wholesaler's fee when determining whether the deal makes financial sense for your project.

Distressed properties, whether due to foreclosure, financial hardship, or neglect, are also prime candidates for flipping. These homes often need extensive renovations, which means they can be bought at a lower price. The challenge with distressed properties is assessing the true cost of repairs. Be prepared to invest in a thorough inspection to avoid surprises that could eat into your profit margin.

The key to sourcing great deals is to remain patient and flexible. Not every deal will be perfect, but with persistence and a keen eye for value, you'll be able to find properties that set you up for success. Whether you're searching through the MLS, attending auctions, or networking for off-market opportunities, the more avenues you explore, the more likely you are to uncover the deal that works for you.

Home Inspection Checklist

Address:
Date:
Note: This checklist is for personal use only. It should not be used in place of an official home inspection. This list may not be comprehensive. Contact a qualified ASHI certified home inspector for an official inspection.

M - missing, S - scratched, D - damaged, B - broken, R - repair/replace, W - Water Damage, L - Leaking

Exterior	Good	OK	Bad
Back Doors			
Deck, porch, patio			
Doorbell			
Driveway			
Front Doors			
Garage Doors			
Garbage receptacle			
House number			
Mailbox			
Outdoor lights			
Paint and trim			
Parking			
Recycling receptacle			
Sidewalks			
Siding (brick/stone/cement)			
Traffic noise			
Windows			

Are things loose, cracked, damaged, rotted, bug infested?
Notes:

Roof	Good	OK	Bad
Chimney			
Gutters and downspouts			
Soffits and fascia			

When was it replaced last? Are there encroaching trees?
Notes:

Garage	Good	OK	Bad
Ceiling			
Doors			
Floors			
Lights			
Storage			
Walls			
Windows			

Is the garage door opener operating properly?
Notes:

Checklist Covering the Exterior, Roof, Garage, and Structural Elements. Source: exceltmp.com

Evaluating Properties for Flipping

One of the most important steps in flipping houses is knowing how to evaluate a property properly. Not every house is a good candidate for a flip, and making the wrong choice can lead to wasted time and lost money. To succeed, you need to know how to spot the right opportunities and avoid the ones that look promising but could turn into a financial trap.

Start by looking at the location. The saying "location, location, location" is as true for house flipping as it is for any other real estate investment. A house in a desirable neighborhood, close to good schools, shopping, and public transportation, will always have more potential than a home in an area with declining property values. Even if you find a house with a low price, it won't matter if the neighborhood is unattractive to buyers. Check local market trends to see if property values are rising, and make sure the area is one where homes are selling quickly.

Next, assess the condition of the property. Look beyond cosmetic issues like outdated paint or worn carpets. Focus on the structural aspects of the house, such as the foundation, roof, plumbing, and electrical systems. If any of these major components need repair or replacement, it can drastically affect your budget and timeline. Cosmetic fixes are much easier and less expensive than dealing with foundational issues or major systems, so be sure to get a thorough inspection before committing to a purchase.

Consider the layout of the house as well. Modern buyers often prefer open-concept layouts and functional, flowing spaces. If the house you're looking at has a cramped or awkward layout, think about whether it can be easily reconfigured to meet current design trends. Sometimes, opening up a few walls can make a huge difference in the appeal of the home, but in other cases, structural changes may be too costly or complicated.

Another key factor to evaluate is the potential resale value. You need to know what similar properties in the area are selling for to determine whether the investment is worth it. Look at comparable sales, or "comps," to get an idea of what the house could sell for once it's renovated. These comps should be similar in size, style, and location to the property you're considering. If the numbers don't add up, even the best renovation won't help you turn a profit.

Finally, consider the cost of the flip. This includes the purchase price, renovation costs, holding costs, and any additional fees associated with the transaction. Once you have a clear picture of the total investment, compare it to the potential resale value. The general rule is that you should aim for a 70% return on investment. That means the purchase price and renovation costs should not exceed 70% of the estimated resale value. This rule gives you a buffer to account for unexpected expenses and ensures you'll walk away with a profit.

By evaluating these key factors—location, condition, layout, resale potential, and costs—you can make informed decisions about which properties are worth pursuing and which ones are better left alone. Successful flipping starts with choosing the right property, and taking the time to evaluate each opportunity carefully will increase your chances of a profitable investment.

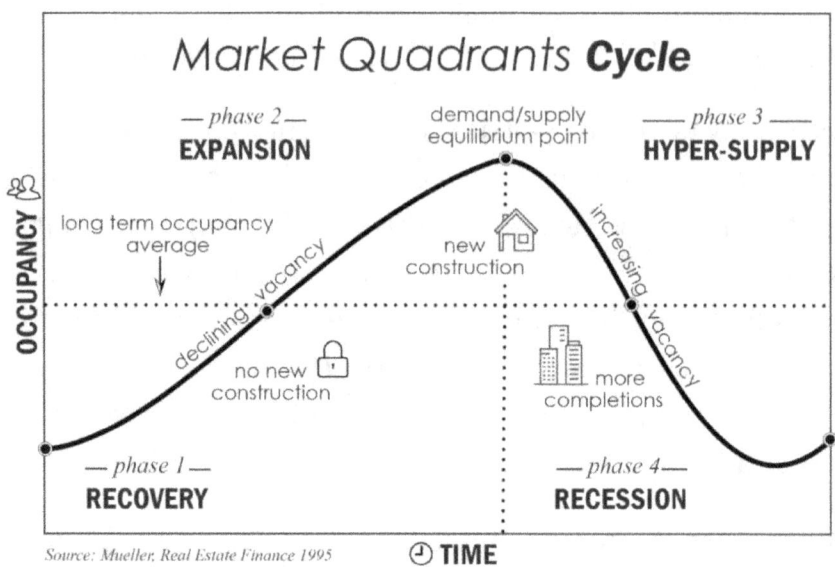

Real Estate Market Cycle Explained. Source: thebrokerlist.com

Avoiding Common Mistakes When Buying

Buying the right property is the foundation of a successful flip. However, there are several common mistakes that can quickly turn a promising project into a financial headache. Knowing what to avoid can save you time, money, and a lot of frustration.

One of the most frequent mistakes new flippers make is overpaying for a property. It's easy to get excited when you find what seems like a great house in a good location, but if you pay too much upfront, you'll have very little room for profit later. The key is to approach every deal with a strict budget in mind. You should calculate the maximum amount you can afford to pay for the property based on its current value, the estimated renovation costs, and the expected resale price. Stick to this number and avoid getting caught up in bidding wars or emotional decisions that could lead to overpaying.

Another common pitfall is underestimating the cost of repairs. What may seem like minor cosmetic issues at first glance can sometimes hide bigger problems, like faulty plumbing or structural damage. It's crucial to get a thorough inspection before making an offer. An experienced contractor or home inspector can help identify hidden issues that might not be obvious during a walkthrough. Skipping this step can lead to expensive surprises once renovations begin, which could severely impact your budget and timeline.

Choosing the wrong location is another mistake that can make or break a flip. Even the most beautifully renovated home will struggle to sell if it's in an undesirable neighborhood. Before buying, spend time researching the area. Look at comparable homes in the neighborhood, crime rates, and the overall trend of the local market. Is the area improving, or is it in decline? Make sure you understand the demand for homes in that specific location, as this will directly impact how quickly and for how much you can sell the property.

Another issue to watch for is not accounting for holding costs. When you buy a property, you'll have ongoing expenses until the day you sell it. These include property taxes, insurance, utilities, and any interest on loans you took to finance the purchase. Many new flippers focus only on the cost of buying and renovating the house, forgetting that every month they hold onto the property eats into their profits. To avoid this, factor holding costs into your budget from the beginning and aim to complete and sell the property as quickly as possible.

Finally, trying to do everything yourself can lead to costly delays and mistakes. While it may be tempting to save money by handling repairs or renovations on your own, it's often better to hire professionals for tasks that require expertise. If you lack experience in a particular area, doing it yourself can lead to subpar results that might cost more to fix later. Knowing when to bring in skilled contractors can save you time and ensure that the work is done right the first time.

Avoiding these common mistakes will help you set the stage for a smoother, more profitable flip. It's all about careful planning, thorough research, and staying disciplined with your budget. With the right approach, you can make smart buying decisions that increase your chances of success.

Chapter 5

The Renovation Process

Creating a Renovation Plan

Once you've secured a property, the next crucial step is creating a solid renovation plan. A well-thought-out plan not only ensures that the project stays on track but also helps you control costs and timelines. It's the roadmap that guides the entire flipping process, from demolition to final touches.

Start by assessing what needs to be done. Walk through the property with a critical eye, identifying areas that need attention. Break the house down into categories such as structural repairs, electrical and plumbing updates, and cosmetic improvements. Prioritize the must-fix issues first. For example, if the roof is leaking or the foundation needs repair, these should be tackled before thinking about paint colors or kitchen upgrades. Safety and structural integrity always come first in any renovation plan.

Once you've determined the scope of work, it's time to set a budget. A renovation budget should be realistic and include everything from major fixes to small details. Include materials, labor, and any permits you'll need. It's also wise to add a cushion for unexpected costs, as surprises are common in any renovation project. Having a clear budget in place helps prevent overspending and keeps the project financially viable.

Next, create a timeline for the renovations. Time is money when flipping houses, so the faster you can complete the work, the better. However, it's important to be realistic about how long each phase of the project will take. Rushing can lead to mistakes, but unnecessary delays can eat into your profits. Break the project down into phases, such as demolition, repairs, painting, and finishing touches, and set specific deadlines for each phase. This keeps the project organized and allows you to track progress effectively.

Communication is key when you're working with contractors or a renovation team. Make sure everyone involved understands the plan, including the budget and timeline. Clearly communicate your expectations, and hold regular check-ins to make sure everything is on track. If something changes along the way, such as unexpected repairs or delays in materials, adjust the plan accordingly and keep the lines of communication open.

Finally, always keep your target buyer in mind as you plan your renovations. The goal is to create a home that will appeal to buyers in the local market, so focus on upgrades that add value. This could mean choosing neutral colors for paint, updating kitchens and bathrooms, or investing in energy-efficient appliances. A renovation that appeals to the most buyers will help your property sell faster and for a higher price.

With a clear renovation plan in place, you can move forward with confidence, knowing that each step is contributing to a successful flip.

Working with Contractors

Finding the right contractor is one of the most important parts of a successful house flip. A skilled contractor can make the renovation process smoother and help you stay on schedule and within budget. However, working with the wrong one can lead to delays, unexpected costs, and headaches. Learning how to manage this relationship effectively is key to a profitable flip.

Start by thoroughly vetting any contractor you're considering. Ask for references and take the time to check their past work. Talking to previous clients can give you a good idea of the contractor's reliability, quality of work, and how well they handle issues that arise during a project. It's also important to verify that they are licensed and insured. A licensed contractor is more likely to meet local building codes, and insurance protects you in case of accidents or damages on the job.

Once you've found a contractor, clear communication is essential. From the very beginning, make sure you're on the same page about the scope of the project, the timeline, and the budget. Be as specific as possible when discussing what you want to achieve with the renovation. Vague instructions can lead to misunderstandings that cost both time and money. If possible, put everything in writing. A detailed contract that outlines the work to be done, payment schedules, and deadlines can help avoid disputes later on.

During the renovation process, it's important to maintain regular communication. You don't need to be on-site every day, but you should check in frequently to ensure the work is progressing as planned. If problems or delays arise, addressing them early can prevent larger issues down the road. Open and honest communication fosters a better working relationship and helps ensure that the project stays on track.

One of the challenges of working with contractors is balancing quality with cost. While it may be tempting to go with the lowest bid, this can sometimes lead to poor-quality work or delays as the contractor takes on other jobs to make up for the low price. It's worth paying a little more for a contractor with a solid reputation who you trust to do the job right. That said, it's still important to negotiate and ensure that the pricing is fair and within your budget.

Finally, make sure to establish a payment schedule that aligns with the progress of the project. It's common practice to pay a portion upfront, with additional payments made as certain milestones are completed. This helps protect you from paying too much before the work is done and ensures the contractor has an incentive to keep the project moving forward.

Working with contractors can be one of the most challenging aspects of flipping houses, but with the right approach, it can also be one of the most rewarding. The goal is to build a partnership where both parties are committed to the successful completion of the project. Trust, communication, and clear expectations are the foundation of that partnership.

DIY vs. Professional Work

When it comes to flipping houses, one of the key decisions you'll face is whether to handle certain tasks yourself or hire a professional. It can be tempting to take the do-it-yourself approach, especially if you're trying to save money. However, it's important to weigh the pros and cons carefully before deciding which tasks to tackle on your own.

DIY projects can offer significant cost savings, especially for tasks that don't require specialized skills. Painting, installing basic fixtures, landscaping, and even some demolition work are areas where many flippers choose to go the DIY route. If you have the time and some basic skills, handling these tasks yourself can reduce labor costs and allow you to put more money into other parts of the project. DIY work also gives you a greater sense of control over the timeline, as you're not waiting for contractors to fit you into their schedule.

That said, it's essential to know your limits. Certain tasks require a level of expertise and precision that most homeowners don't possess. Electrical work, plumbing, roofing, and structural repairs are best left to licensed professionals. Not only can mistakes in these areas lead to safety hazards, but they can also cost you more in the long run if the work has to be redone or fails to pass inspection. For example, improper wiring can cause electrical fires, while faulty plumbing can result in water damage that eats into your profits. Hiring a professional ensures the job is done right and up to code, which is crucial when it's time to sell the property.

Time is another important factor to consider. DIY projects can often take longer than expected, especially if you're juggling multiple tasks or working around other responsibilities. While saving on labor costs is appealing, a project that drags on because you're doing everything yourself can hurt your bottom line. The longer the property sits unfinished, the more you'll pay in holding costs like mortgage payments, taxes, and utilities. Sometimes, it's more cost-effective to hire a professional who can complete the work quickly and efficiently, freeing you up to focus on other parts of the flip.

Quality is also something to keep in mind. Buyers will be looking closely at the details when they tour your flip, and sloppy or amateur work can stand out. A poorly installed tile floor or uneven cabinets can turn off potential buyers and lower the perceived value of the home. If a task requires a high level of craftsmanship or if you're aiming for a polished, professional look, it's worth paying for a pro to get the job done right.

In the end, it's about finding the right balance. Some projects are perfect for DIY, especially if they're simple, straightforward, and don't pose safety risks. Others are better left to professionals who can ensure the work is done to a high standard and within a reasonable timeframe. By knowing where to draw the line, you can maximize your budget while still delivering a top-quality finished product that attracts buyers.

Chapter 6

Selling for Maximum Profit

Staging Your Home to Sell Fast

Staging a home is a crucial step in the selling process, especially when you're looking to sell quickly. The goal of staging is to make the property as appealing as possible to potential buyers, helping them envision themselves living in the space. A well-staged home not only looks better in photos but can also create an emotional connection that motivates buyers to make an offer.

Staged Living Room. Source: flux-image.com

The first step in staging is creating a clean, clutter-free environment. Buyers want to see the home, not your stuff. Remove any personal items, excess furniture, and knick-knacks. Clear surfaces like countertops, coffee tables, and shelves to create a sense of space and openness. The fewer distractions there are, the easier it is for potential buyers to imagine their own belongings in the home. A clean, minimalist look also makes the rooms appear larger and more inviting.

Neutralizing the space is another key element of staging. Bold colors or highly personalized décor can turn off some buyers, so it's best to keep things neutral. Repaint any bright or unusual walls in light, neutral tones like beige, gray, or soft whites. These colors help create a blank canvas that appeals to a broader audience. Similarly, keep the furniture and décor simple and tasteful, aiming for a style that complements the home without overpowering it.

Lighting plays a major role in how a home feels. Bright, natural light is always a selling point, so open curtains and blinds to let in as much sunlight as possible. If certain areas of the home don't get much natural light, use lamps and light fixtures to brighten things up. A well-lit home feels more welcoming and can make rooms look bigger and more attractive.

Pay special attention to key rooms like the kitchen, living room, and master bedroom. These are often the spaces that buyers focus on the most. In the kitchen, clear the countertops and add a few decorative touches, like a bowl of fresh fruit or a vase of flowers. In the living room, arrange the furniture to create a comfortable, conversational layout. The master bedroom should feel like a peaceful retreat, with fresh bedding and neatly arranged furniture. These small touches can make a big difference in how buyers perceive the space.

Don't forget about curb appeal, as the exterior is the first thing buyers will see. Make sure the yard is well-maintained, with trimmed grass and tidy landscaping. Add some potted plants or flowers near the front entrance to create a welcoming feel. A fresh coat of paint on the front door or new hardware can give the house an instant facelift.

Curb Appeal Enhancements. Source: okchomesellers.com

Staging doesn't have to be expensive or complicated, but it can have a big impact on how quickly your home sells. The goal is to present the home in its best light, highlighting its strengths and helping buyers see its full potential. With the right staging, you can create an environment that attracts interest and leads to a faster sale.

Pricing Your Flip

One of the most important decisions you'll make during the flipping process is determining the right price for your finished property. Pricing your flip correctly can make all the difference between a quick sale and a house that lingers on the market. It requires a careful balance—price too high, and you may scare off potential buyers; price too low, and you leave money on the table.

Start by doing a thorough market analysis. Look at comparable homes, or "comps," in the area that have recently sold. These homes should be similar to your flip in terms of size, style, and condition. This gives you a realistic idea of what buyers in your area are willing to pay for a home like yours. Pay close attention to the sale prices, not just the listing prices. What homes actually sell for provides the best indication of market value.

Next, consider the unique features of your property. If you've added significant upgrades, such as a modern kitchen or high-end finishes, you might be able to price your flip higher than other homes in the neighborhood. On the other hand, if your flip lacks certain desirable features, like a garage or a large yard, you may need to price it slightly lower to stay competitive. The key is to be objective and realistic about your home's strengths and weaknesses in comparison to others on the market.

Timing also plays a big role in pricing. The real estate market can fluctuate throughout the year, and understanding the timing of your sale is important. If you're selling during a hot market, where demand outweighs supply, you might be able to price your flip more aggressively. However, in slower markets or during off-peak seasons, you may need to adjust your price downward to attract interest.

It's also crucial to consider your carrying costs. The longer your flip sits on the market, the more you'll spend on things like mortgage payments, insurance, and property taxes. These ongoing costs can chip away at your profits. In some cases, it might make sense to price the property slightly lower to ensure a quicker sale, rather than holding out for the highest possible price and facing additional holding costs.

When setting your price, keep in mind that buyers are savvy and often do their own research before making an offer. An overpriced home can lead to fewer showings and prolonged time on the market, which might ultimately force you to lower the price later. This can hurt your position in negotiations, as buyers may perceive the price reduction as a sign of desperation. Pricing competitively from the start can generate more interest and even lead to multiple offers, potentially driving up the final sale price.

Pricing your flip isn't just about covering your costs and making a profit; it's also about understanding the market dynamics, your property's value, and buyer expectations. When done right, a well-priced flip can sell quickly, allowing you to move on to your next project with confidence.

Working with Real Estate Agents

Partnering with the right real estate agent can make a significant difference in the success of your house flip. An experienced agent brings valuable market knowledge, negotiation skills, and a network of connections that can help you sell your property quickly and for the best possible price.

When choosing a real estate agent, it's important to find someone who understands the specific needs of house flippers. Not every agent specializes in investment properties, so look for one with experience in buying and selling homes that have been renovated. An agent who knows the local market well can help you set a competitive price, attract the right buyers, and navigate the selling process smoothly.

Communication is key when working with an agent. From the beginning, make sure you are both clear on your goals for the sale. Discuss your desired timeline and any pricing expectations. A good agent will give you honest feedback about the market and help you make informed decisions, but they also need to understand your priorities. Keeping an open line of communication throughout the process ensures that you're on the same page and can address any issues as they arise.

Another advantage of working with a skilled agent is their ability to market your property effectively. In addition to listing your home on the MLS, agents often have access to a wide range of marketing tools. This can include professional photography, virtual tours, and social media promotions. An agent with strong marketing skills will know how to highlight the best features of your home to attract the attention of potential buyers. They can also tap into their network of contacts, including other agents and buyers, to generate interest in the property.

Negotiation is another area where a real estate agent can be invaluable. When offers start coming in, your agent will help you evaluate them, ensuring you get the best deal possible. They'll be able to guide you through the negotiation process, advising on when to make counteroffers or accept a buyer's terms. This can be especially helpful if you're balancing multiple offers or dealing with contingencies in a contract.

A strong agent will also manage the details of the closing process. From handling the paperwork to coordinating with inspectors and appraisers, they take care of the logistical aspects so you can focus on your next project. Their expertise can help prevent delays or legal issues that could otherwise complicate the sale.

Working with a real estate agent is about building a partnership. The right agent can not only help you sell your current flip but also become a valuable asset for future projects. By finding someone who understands your goals and knows the market, you can maximize your chances of selling quickly and profitably.

Chapter 7

Advanced Strategies for Scaling Your Business

Transitioning from Hobbyist to Professional Flipper

Moving from a part-time flipper to a full-time professional requires a shift in mindset, strategy, and commitment. While flipping a house or two on the side can be a fun and profitable hobby, turning it into a sustainable business demands a more structured approach.

The first step in this transition is treating your flips like a business. This means setting clear goals, creating detailed budgets, and sticking to timelines. When flipping is a hobby, there's more room for flexibility, but as a professional, you need to stay organized and efficient. Each decision you make should be calculated to maximize profit and minimize risk. You'll also want to track your expenses closely, keeping detailed records of each project to better understand where your money is going and how you can improve profitability in future flips.

Another key element of becoming a professional flipper is building a reliable network of experts. As a hobbyist, you might have handled many tasks yourself or called on friends and family for help. But as you scale up, it's essential to have a trusted team of contractors, real estate agents, inspectors, and lenders. These professionals can help you streamline the process, save time, and avoid costly mistakes. Having a dependable team allows you to take on more projects without spreading yourself too thin, making it possible to handle multiple flips at once.

Efficiency becomes even more important when you're flipping houses full-time. You need to get comfortable with delegating tasks to your team and focusing on the bigger picture—finding deals, managing the budget, and ensuring each project stays on track. This might mean stepping back from hands-on work like painting or small repairs and focusing on overseeing the renovation as a whole. By shifting your role from worker to manager, you can increase your output and scale your business.

Financing also takes on a new level of importance. As a hobbyist, you might have financed one or two flips with personal savings or a small loan, but a professional flipper often needs access to larger and more flexible funding. Developing strong relationships with lenders and private investors can give you the financial backing to take on bigger projects or multiple flips at once. Understanding how to leverage financing to grow your business is crucial as you move into professional flipping.

Marketing and selling your flips efficiently is another area where professionals differ from hobbyists. Rather than relying on word of mouth or waiting for buyers to come to you, a professional flipper actively markets properties to generate interest and drive faster sales. This includes working with skilled real estate agents, creating appealing listings, and even investing in staging or high-quality photography to present the home in its best light. The faster you can sell each property, the sooner you can move on to the next project, boosting your overall return on investment.

Finally, transitioning to professional flipping requires a long-term vision. As a hobbyist, each flip might feel like an isolated project, but professionals think about the bigger picture—building a brand, expanding their portfolio, and increasing their market presence. This shift in perspective helps you not only survive in the competitive world of flipping but thrive as you grow your reputation and business over time.

Building a Team of Experts

Flipping houses is not a solo endeavor. To be successful, you need to surround yourself with a team of experts who can help you navigate the many aspects of a flip. Each member of your team plays a vital role in ensuring the project runs smoothly, stays on budget, and ultimately leads to a profitable sale.

The foundation of your team starts with a skilled real estate agent. A good agent knows the local market, understands what buyers are looking for, and can guide you to properties with potential. They'll also help you set a competitive selling price when it's time to list the house and market it effectively to attract buyers. Working with an agent who has experience in investment properties is key, as they will be more attuned to the needs and timelines of house flippers.

Next, you'll need a reliable contractor. Renovations are at the heart of house flipping, and having a contractor you can trust to deliver quality work on time and within budget is crucial. It's important to vet contractors carefully, checking their previous work and references. A strong relationship with a contractor means you can collaborate on future projects, building efficiency into each flip as you learn how to work together effectively.

An experienced home inspector is another critical member of your team. They'll help you identify potential problems with a property before you commit to buying it. An inspector's trained eye can spot issues like foundation problems, electrical concerns, or hidden water damage that could turn a seemingly good deal into a money pit. Having a home inspector you trust will give you peace of mind that you're making informed decisions.

In addition to your core team, it's also beneficial to have a dependable accountant. Flipping houses has tax implications that can get complicated, especially if you're flipping multiple properties. A knowledgeable accountant can help you manage your finances, track expenses, and ensure that you're complying with tax regulations. They can also advise you on ways to maximize your profits by taking advantage of deductions and other financial strategies.

Finally, consider adding a property manager to your team if you plan to hold onto properties as rentals after flipping. A property manager can take care of day-to-day tasks like screening tenants, handling maintenance requests, and collecting rent, allowing you to focus on your next project.

Building a strong team is an investment in your success. The right experts will not only help you avoid costly mistakes but also make the flipping process more efficient and enjoyable. With a team you can rely on, you'll be able to focus on growing your flipping business and tackling bigger projects with confidence.

Leveraging Technology and Data

In today's real estate market, technology and data play a significant role in helping house flippers make smarter, faster, and more informed decisions. Whether you're searching for the right property, managing a renovation, or pricing your flip for sale, the right tools can streamline your entire process and give you a competitive edge.

One of the most valuable ways technology can help is by providing access to market data. Real estate platforms and apps allow you to analyze local markets, track property values, and compare recent sales in a matter of minutes. This kind of data was once available only to real estate agents, but now you can access detailed information about neighborhood trends, property taxes, and price fluctuations from the comfort of your phone or computer. By using these tools, you can quickly identify which areas are growing and where you're likely to get the best return on your investment.

Property analysis tools are also essential. Many apps and software programs are designed specifically for investors and flippers, offering features like deal calculators that allow you to estimate costs, profits, and risks before you make an offer. These platforms can help you calculate potential renovation expenses, factor in holding costs, and predict what a property will sell for after improvements. With this level of detail at your fingertips, you can avoid costly surprises and make more accurate financial decisions from the start.

Technology also improves how you manage the renovation process. Project management apps allow you to keep track of your budget, schedule, and tasks all in one place, ensuring that everything stays on track. These tools are particularly useful when you're juggling multiple projects or working with a team of contractors. You can assign tasks, set deadlines, and monitor progress in real-time, reducing the chances of delays and miscommunications. Keeping everything organized in one system also allows you to look back at past projects to see where improvements can be made in future flips.

Data-driven marketing is another area where technology shines. Listing platforms, social media, and real estate websites make it easier than ever to reach potential buyers. You can create detailed, visually appealing listings, use targeted ads to reach specific buyer demographics, and track how your listing is performing online. High-quality photos, virtual tours, and drone footage give buyers a closer look at your property, attracting more interest and helping your flip stand out in a competitive market. Many platforms even offer insights into how many people are viewing your listing and how long properties typically take to sell in your area, giving you real-time feedback on your pricing and marketing strategy.

The power of technology in flipping houses goes beyond just finding properties and marketing them. It gives you the tools to make data-driven decisions at every stage of the process. From analyzing a property's potential to optimizing your renovation plan and attracting buyers, leveraging technology allows you to work smarter and more efficiently, giving you an advantage in a fast-paced and competitive industry.

Property Management Dashboard. Source: boldbi.com

Chapter 8

Legal and Tax Considerations

Legal Issues in House Flipping

Flipping houses can be a profitable venture, but it comes with a range of legal responsibilities and challenges. Understanding the legal landscape is crucial to avoid complications that could derail your project or reduce your profits. By staying informed and proactive, you can navigate these issues smoothly and protect yourself from potential legal trouble.

One of the first legal matters to address is ensuring that you have the proper permits for any renovations or construction work. Different cities and municipalities have their own regulations, and failing to obtain the right permits can lead to fines, delays, or even having to undo completed work. Whether you're doing structural changes, electrical upgrades, or plumbing, it's important to check local building codes and secure the necessary permits before starting any project. A good contractor should be familiar with the permitting process, but ultimately, the responsibility falls on you as the property owner to ensure compliance.

Zoning laws are another important legal consideration. Each property is subject to zoning restrictions that dictate how it can be used. For example, a property may be zoned for residential, commercial, or mixed-use purposes. If you're planning to make significant changes to a property, such as converting a multi-family unit into a single-family home, you'll need to ensure that the zoning regulations allow for that type of modification. Violating zoning laws can result in penalties and may force you to revert the property to its original condition.

Contracts are also a central part of the house-flipping process. From buying the property to hiring contractors, each step of the flip involves legal agreements. It's essential to carefully review and understand any contracts before signing. When purchasing a property, make sure you are clear on the terms of the sale, including contingencies related to inspections or financing. Similarly, contractor agreements should outline the scope of work, payment schedules, and deadlines. If something goes wrong, having a solid contract in place can protect you and give you legal recourse.

Another important legal issue is property disclosures. When it comes time to sell the property, you are legally required to disclose any known defects or issues with the home. This could include things like mold, structural damage, or a history of flooding. Failing to disclose known problems can lead to lawsuits from the buyer after the sale is completed. It's best to be transparent about any issues and fix them before listing the property, or at the very least, make sure potential buyers are aware.

Tax laws are another area to keep in mind. Flipping houses can result in capital gains taxes, which are taxes on the profit made from selling the property. The amount you owe will depend on how long you've owned the property and your overall tax situation. If you flip multiple properties in a short period, you might also be considered a business by the IRS, which can change your tax liabilities. It's a good idea to consult with a tax professional who can help you navigate these rules and ensure that you're properly reporting your income.

Lastly, consider the possibility of liability issues. If someone is injured on the property during the renovation process, you could be held responsible. Make sure that your contractor has proper insurance and that you have liability coverage to protect yourself in case of accidents. Additionally, hiring licensed and insured contractors can help minimize the risk of legal problems related to workmanship or safety.

Flipping houses involves more than just buying, renovating, and selling. By understanding and addressing these legal issues, you can reduce risk, avoid costly mistakes, and protect your investment throughout the process.

Tax Implications

When flipping houses, it's essential to understand the tax implications that come with your profits. Flipping may seem like a straightforward process of buying, renovating, and selling, but taxes can have a significant impact on your overall earnings. Knowing what to expect and how to plan for taxes can help you avoid surprises and keep more of your profits.

First, the way your flip is taxed depends on how long you hold the property. If you sell the property less than a year after purchasing it, the profit is considered short-term capital gains. This means the income is taxed at the same rate as your ordinary income, which could range from 10% to 37%, depending on your total taxable income. Because short-term capital gains are taxed at a higher rate than long-term investments, it's important to factor this into your budget when calculating your potential profits.

On the other hand, if you hold the property for more than a year before selling it, the profit is considered long-term capital gains. Long-term capital gains are taxed at a lower rate, ranging from 0% to 20%, depending on your income level. While holding a property for a longer period could reduce your tax burden, it also increases your holding costs, such as mortgage payments, taxes, and insurance. This means you'll need to weigh the benefits of waiting for a lower tax rate against the extra costs of holding onto the property for an extended time.

In some cases, flipping houses can be considered a business rather than an investment. If you flip multiple properties each year or treat house flipping as your full-time job, the IRS may classify your activity as a business. In this case, your profits would be subject to self-employment taxes in addition to income taxes. Self-employment tax covers Social Security and Medicare contributions, which can add up to an additional 15.3% on top of your regular tax rate. To reduce the impact of self-employment taxes, many professional flippers choose to structure their business as an LLC or corporation, which can provide more flexibility when it comes to tax planning.

Another tax consideration for flippers is capital gains exclusions. If the property you're flipping is also your primary residence and you've lived there for at least two of the last five years, you may be eligible for a capital gains exclusion. This exclusion allows single filers to exclude up to $250,000 of profit from capital gains taxes, while married couples filing jointly can exclude up to $500,000. However, this benefit applies only if the property is your primary residence, so it may not be relevant for most flips, which are usually investment properties.

Finally, don't forget about deductible expenses. Many of the costs associated with flipping houses, such as renovation expenses, materials, contractor fees, and even marketing costs, may be tax-deductible. Keeping detailed records of all your expenses throughout the project is crucial. These deductions can help lower your taxable income, reducing the amount of tax you owe at the end of the year.

Understanding the tax implications of flipping houses is key to protecting your profits. With proper planning and record-keeping, you can minimize your tax burden and keep more of your earnings while staying compliant with tax laws.

When Flipping Becomes a Business

Flipping houses can start as a side project, but for many, it evolves into a full-fledged business. If you've successfully completed a few flips and are thinking about scaling up, it's important to recognize when your hobby has transitioned into a business and what that means for how you operate.

One of the key indicators that flipping has become more than just a personal project is the frequency of your deals. If you're flipping multiple properties in a short amount of time, it's likely that the IRS and local authorities will start to view your activities as a business rather than an investment. This shift means you'll need to take steps to formalize your operations, including properly registering your business and handling taxes in a way that reflects your new status. Consulting with a tax professional or accountant can help you understand when flipping qualifies as a business for tax purposes, which impacts how you report income, pay taxes, and manage deductions.

Another sign that your flipping has become a business is the level of organization required to keep things running smoothly. As you flip more properties, managing the day-to-day tasks of multiple projects can become overwhelming. This is where it becomes essential to set up systems to streamline your operations. You may need to create workflows for budgeting, hiring contractors, sourcing materials, and selling properties. The more organized your process, the easier it will be to handle multiple projects at once, keeping timelines and costs under control.

At this stage, it's also worth considering the benefits of setting up a legal entity, such as an LLC (Limited Liability Company). An LLC provides personal liability protection, meaning that if something goes wrong with a flip—like a lawsuit or a significant financial loss—your personal assets won't be at risk. Creating a legal entity also adds credibility to your business and can make it easier to secure financing from lenders who prefer working with established businesses rather than individuals.

As your flipping business grows, you may also need to bring on additional help. This could mean hiring employees, such as project managers, or outsourcing tasks like accounting and marketing. Building a team allows you to focus on the big-picture aspects of the business, like finding deals and expanding your operations, while leaving the day-to-day details to trusted professionals. Managing people is a new responsibility, but having the right team in place can significantly improve your efficiency and ability to scale.

When flipping becomes a business, your approach to financing will also change. In the beginning, you might have used personal savings or small loans to fund your flips. But as your business grows, you'll likely need more significant, consistent funding. Establishing relationships with lenders who specialize in real estate investment can help you secure the capital needed to take on larger projects. Additionally, as a business, you might explore alternative financing options such as business lines of credit, private investors, or partnerships with other real estate professionals.

Another critical shift is in your mindset. Running a flipping business requires you to think long-term. You'll need to focus not just on each individual deal, but also on building a brand, developing a reputation, and ensuring steady growth over time. This might involve expanding into new markets, diversifying the types of properties you flip, or even branching out into rental properties or new construction. The key is to have a clear strategy for the future, one that includes setting goals, tracking performance, and continuously improving your processes.

Flipping houses as a business can be incredibly rewarding, offering both financial success and personal satisfaction. But it requires a more formal approach, from how you handle taxes to how you structure your operations. Recognizing when flipping has evolved into a business allows you to make the necessary adjustments and set yourself up for long-term success.

Chapter 9

Common Pitfalls and How to Avoid Them

Overestimating Profit Margins

One of the most common mistakes new house flippers make is overestimating profit margins. It's easy to get excited about a project and imagine the large profits you'll make once the renovations are complete and the house sells. However, it's crucial to approach each flip with a realistic understanding of the costs involved and the potential return. Overestimating how much money you'll make can lead to disappointment—or worse, financial losses.

The first area where flippers often overestimate profits is in the resale price of the home. It's tempting to believe that every improvement you make will significantly increase the property's value, but the market ultimately determines how much a buyer is willing to pay. Overpricing a home can result in it sitting on the market longer than expected, increasing your holding costs and eating into your profits. Instead of assuming the highest possible sale price, it's better to base your expectations on comparable sales in the area and price the property competitively.

Another place where profits are often overestimated is in underestimating renovation costs. Even with a solid renovation plan in place, unexpected expenses frequently arise. Hidden issues like electrical problems, plumbing repairs, or foundation cracks can quickly add thousands of dollars to your budget. It's important to leave room for these surprises by padding your budget with a contingency fund. Assuming everything will go smoothly can set you up for financial trouble when things don't go as planned.

Additionally, holding costs are often overlooked when calculating profit margins. These are the ongoing expenses you'll need to pay while you own the property, such as mortgage payments, property taxes, insurance, and utilities. The longer the property takes to sell, the more these costs accumulate. Many flippers focus on renovation costs and the sale price, forgetting that holding costs can significantly reduce their overall profit, especially if the market is slow or the property doesn't sell right away.

Finally, transaction fees and taxes can further reduce your profit. Real estate commissions, closing costs, and capital gains taxes all need to be factored in when calculating your expected return. These fees can take a sizable chunk out of your profit if you haven't accounted for them in advance.

Being realistic about profit margins means carefully accounting for all potential costs and setting conservative expectations for the sale price. While flipping can be profitable, approaching each project with a clear understanding of the financial risks and rewards will help ensure your success over the long term.

Market Fluctuations

Market fluctuations are a reality that every house flipper must face. The real estate market, like any market, is influenced by a variety of factors—economic conditions, interest rates, and even seasonal trends. These shifts can impact everything from the price you pay for a property to how long it takes to sell after renovations are complete. Understanding and navigating these fluctuations is key to maintaining profitability in your flips.

One of the most obvious signs of a fluctuating market is the rise and fall of home prices. During a hot market, prices climb quickly as demand exceeds supply. This can make it harder to find affordable properties to flip, but on the flip side, you may be able to sell your renovated home for a higher price. In a slow market, prices tend to drop, meaning you might find great deals on homes. However, selling the property could take longer, and you might need to adjust your expectations on the final sale price. Keeping a close eye on local housing trends can help you anticipate these changes and adjust your strategy accordingly.

Interest rates also play a major role in market conditions. When interest rates are low, buyers are more likely to take out mortgages, driving demand and pushing home prices higher. On the other hand, when interest rates rise, borrowing becomes more expensive, which can lead to a slowdown in the market. For flippers, this can mean longer holding periods and increased pressure to reduce prices in order to attract buyers. Monitoring interest rate trends and understanding their effect on buyer behavior can help you time your projects more effectively.

Another factor to consider is the seasonality of the real estate market. The housing market tends to be more active in spring and summer when families are looking to move before the start of a new school year. Conversely, winter months often see a slowdown in activity, as fewer people are willing to buy or sell during the holiday season. If you're flipping a house, it's important to factor in these seasonal patterns when planning your renovation schedule. Selling during the more active months can increase your chances of a quicker sale at a favorable price.

Market fluctuations can also be driven by broader economic conditions. In times of economic growth, consumer confidence rises, and more people are willing to invest in real estate. During economic downturns, however, buyers may become more cautious, leading to lower demand for homes and slower sales. While these larger trends are beyond your control, staying informed about the overall economy can help you anticipate potential changes in the market and adjust your approach.

Ultimately, the key to navigating market fluctuations is flexibility. A successful house flipper knows how to adapt to changing conditions. Whether that means adjusting your budget, changing your renovation strategy, or being patient in a slower market, understanding the forces at play allows you to make informed decisions and stay profitable, even in uncertain times.

Staying Emotionally Detached

When flipping houses, one of the hardest yet most important things to do is stay emotionally detached from the property. It's natural to become invested in a project, especially when you're pouring time, effort, and creativity into transforming a house. However, allowing emotions to influence your decisions can lead to costly mistakes that impact your bottom line.

At its core, flipping is a business. The goal is to make a profit by buying, renovating, and selling a property. While it's tempting to personalize a flip with design choices that reflect your own style or preferences, you have to remember that you're not the one who will be living in the house. It's crucial to make design decisions that appeal to the broadest range of potential buyers.

Neutral colors, classic finishes, and modern features that are in line with current market trends will often yield better results than bold, personal design choices.

Getting emotionally attached can also lead to overspending. When you're passionate about a project, it's easy to justify spending more than you planned, whether it's upgrading fixtures or adding features you think would "complete" the home. However, every dollar you spend eats into your profit margin. It's important to stick to your budget and remember that not every upgrade will translate to a higher sale price. Make decisions based on what will provide the best return on investment, not what feels most exciting or impressive.

Another way emotions can interfere is during negotiations. Selling a flip can be stressful, and it's common to feel attached to the final product after all the hard work that's gone into it. However, getting too attached can make it difficult to negotiate objectively with potential buyers. If you've fallen in love with the home or are overly proud of your renovation, you might set an unrealistic price or refuse reasonable offers, resulting in the property sitting on the market longer than expected. The key is to focus on the numbers and keep the sale process as businesslike as possible.

Ultimately, staying emotionally detached allows you to make smart, rational decisions throughout the flipping process. By keeping a clear focus on your budget, design choices, and the market, you'll be better positioned to achieve your financial goals and move on to your next successful flip.

Conclusion

Flipping houses, when done right, offers an incredible opportunity to build wealth, express creativity, and make a tangible impact on the real estate market. Throughout this book, we've covered the essential steps to take your flipping business from an idea to a profitable venture. You've learned how to evaluate markets, secure funding, create realistic budgets, and manage renovations with precision. We've explored the importance of staying objective, making data-driven decisions, and keeping a sharp focus on the end goal: maximizing your return on investment.

At the heart of successful flipping is a balance between smart planning and flexibility. You now understand the importance of buying at the right price, managing costs carefully, and delivering a property that speaks to buyers' needs. You've also seen how leveraging technology, staying on top of market trends, and building a solid team can streamline your processes and set you up for long-term success. These strategies are not just for one flip—they're the foundation for growing your flipping business into a sustainable and profitable enterprise.

This journey is as much about mindset as it is about skill. Whether you're transitioning from hobbyist to professional or just starting your first flip, the principles outlined here will guide you through the challenges and rewards of flipping houses. It's a business that demands dedication, but for those willing to commit, the possibilities are immense.

As you move forward, keep these lessons close. Trust your research, stick to your budget, and remember that each flip is a stepping stone toward bigger goals. Most importantly, stay adaptable and ready to learn with each new project. The real estate market will continue to evolve, and the most successful flippers are those who embrace change while holding firm to the core principles of smart investing.

The next step is yours to take. Whether it's purchasing your first flip or scaling your business, you now have the tools and knowledge to make informed decisions and achieve real success. Approach each project with confidence, knowing that with careful planning and a focused mindset, you can turn any property into a profitable investment. Your journey as a professional flipper has just begun.

Dear Reader,

I hope you found the book insightful and valuable.

Your feedback is invaluable to me. If you enjoyed reading this book, I would appreciate it if you could take a moment to leave a review on the reading apps and platforms.

Thank you for your support, and I wish you all the best.

Kind regards,
Ghazwan

About the Author

Ghazwan is a passionate entrepreneur and business strategist dedicated to helping individuals and organizations achieve their full potential with a deep understanding of modern businesses' challenges and opportunities.

With a Master's degree in Computer and Systems Sciences from Stockholm University, specializing in eService design, requirement engineering, and business process management, he is equipped to innovate cutting-edge solutions.

He believes in the power of collaboration and lifelong learning, and his mission is to empower people to reach their goals and positively impact the world.

www.ingramcontent.com/pod-product-compliance
Lightning Source LLC
Chambersburg PA
CBHW071106240526
45469CB00006BD/2353